Handbook

For

Secret Agents

The work of secret agents is not recent. Secret agents have been used from antiquity. The Biblical Joshua used secret agents; Roman emperors too. During and after World War 1 and 2 different countries--Germany, France, the Soviet Union, United States, etc. ---used secret agents against each other. So who is a secret agent?

Contents

A secret agent is a person hired to secretly do a job. The works of secret agents vary.

Some secret agents work solely to protect, such as the secret agents protecting the president of the United States and his family.

Some secret agents are hired killers--assassins, hit man--whose assignments are solely to kill.

Many secret agents only spy.

Some secret agents do all the three things (spy, protect and kill), such as the secret agents operating US drones.

The book, however, is for the secret agents who only spy.

Working

As

A

Spy

Definition

Assignment: A task a spy is hired to carry out.

Client. A government, organization, or private person using the service of a spy.

Code. A system of numbers, letters, symbols or gestures used to represent secret information.

Colleague. Another spy that you work with.

Double agent. An agent who pretends to act as a spy for one part (private person, organization or country) while in fact acting for its enemy.

Eliminate. Kill.

Failed assignment. An assignment a spy did not succeed at accomplishing.

Political espionage. Spying activities of governments.

Political spy. A spy working for a government.

Working as a spy

Your work as a spy is a life of chicanery and dangers. It is a life of walking tight ropes to find information and expose clandestine activities. As a spy, your job is to dig into secrets and pass on what you know to who has hired you--whether it be a government, organization or private person. The three elements of your job as a spy are to:

1.Pretend
2.Fit in
3.Gather information

A fourth element sometimes exists. In some assignments the agent is hired to pretend, fit in, gather information and then to--as the fourth element--purloin, or destroy something.

Starting Out

You can start out as a spy by working for a government, an organization or be self-employed. If you are thinking of working for a government or organization, you may need to have more than just the desire to be a spy. However, it cannot be logical to state any particular skill that you must have to be a spy. Governments and organizations have used children, teens, and even elderly persons as spies throughout history. Some persons were used as secret agents merely because of their ethnicity, their beauty and charm, or merely because of their ordinary lives. So it is not generally a must that you first must have special skills or training. If you don't, the government or organization that hires you will train you.

If you are thinking of being a self-employed agent, you must (if you will offer your service to the public) operate using the term 'private investigator'--not secret agent or spy. No one who works as a spy does that. As a self-employed secret agent, you must advertise your service to the public as a private investigator. And there are some rulers that come with advertising:

1. **Never show your face or the face of your colleague (s).** If you publish your face as a private investigator, you damage your ability to 'privately' investigate. Also never put your face on your business cards, Facebook page or website.

2. **Don't have an open office**. You should not have an office where anyone from the public can just walk in. You should meet all new clients by appointment via assignation--whether the person was referred to you by another spy or replying to your advertisement. Know exactly why the person wants to use your service before the meeting. Get enough information on the person before you meet. Who is the person who wants to use your service? From where? You set the meeting place, not the person. Never meet an anonymous individual.

3. **Never use land line phone numbers in your advertising**. It is wise to use a cell phone number. If you advertise a home or office number, you are offering an easy-to-find road to where you operate from.

4. **State what you can be hired for.** Tell what you can be hired for. You do not have to spell everything out on your business cards or in any other forms of advertisements. You can simply put--for example--"private investigation for companies, private individuals and governments."

Getting Paid

Payment for your job must be taken seriously. You control what you charge, how you must be paid, when you must be paid. You should not put this control in anybody's hand. If you let someone decides what they pay you, how they pay you, and when they pay you--they will regard you, in their minds, as a pushover. This is not to say that you should not leave room for negotiation. There will be persons who will want to use your service but do not have a lot of money. You should try work out a deal that fits their pockets.

The following rules also apply to payment:

1. **Avoid working on a salary.** A secret agent who is a spy or assassin does not work on a salary. If you work for a government or organization, you should negotiate a fixed amount for each assignment plus the necessary support (equipment, weapons, etc.) from the government or organization.

Exception: There are government spies nowadays who exclusively use computer technology to spy. These spies--who normally work from a safe building and do not take personal risks to themselves--usually work on a salary under their contract.

2. **Never start executing an assignment without first getting a portion of your money**--especially if you are self-employed. You will need money, no matter how little or large, to start an assignment. Do not use money from your own pocket and arrange to be reimbursed by the client. You should have a client give you at least 50% of the agreed payment (which must be non-returnable) before you start working. The money is necessary for the self-employed agent to cover expenses that will come with the executing of an assignment--such as, for example, travel, food, equipments. It is really up to you to decide method of payment--cash only, check, wire transfer, etc. It is best to choose the 'cash only' method, especially if your job on behalf of a client is illegitimate or the client is someone you do not want to have a traceable link to.

3. **Never work for cheap money**. A spy does not work for cheap money. But there is a thing called 'bargaining power.' Your bargaining power (how much influence you have to get what you want) is determined on your value. If you are accomplished (such as being an excellent hacker and someone like you cannot be easily found somewhere else) then your bargaining power is high, and so you can ask for the big bucks to do an assignment. If you do not have any special skill or track record (passed successes) then your bargaining power is low, and you will have to go easy on what you charge.

Special note: When others want you, not need you, you cannot charge the big bucks--because they don't have to use your service. When others need you, not want you, then you charge the big bucks--because the person 'need to' use your service.

Personal requirements
to be a
Spy

While the abilities to see, hear and move are sufficient to be a spy, there are some general requirements to be a good spy.

1. **Be willing to take risks.** The life of a spy involves risks. You must be willing to take risks. But never take a risk without having a thought out plan on how you will get in and get out. While you are willing to take risks, you must study all risks to know when a risk is not worth taking by yourself, at a particular time, or not worth taking at all.

2. **Make yourself multi-talented.** The more things you can do, the more jobs you will be hired for. You can increase your abilities by learn how to drive, ride, swim, use phone and computer technologies well. You cannot know everything. So it is judicious to know one or few individuals with special abilities--such as a computer geek who can get around secured computer systems or an excellent document forger--who you can turn to for facilitating an assignment.

3. **Be confidential**. Anyone who considers you to do a job will want to feel that you can be trusted. So be confidential. To be an agent that others can trust, you must never share the information of your clients-- government, organization, or private persons--with anyone. The only exception may be a colleague. The information you get from your clients, and the information you gather for your clients, should be handled confidentially.

4. **Have little or no family liabilities.** If you are the kind of agent whose job takes you away from home--even from your country--for long periods of time, then you may want to have little or no family liabilities.

5. **Avoid being morally strict.** You cannot be a morally strict person while working as a spy. This is because you will have to lie to your family, friends, and others about what you really do for a living. You also have to be a deceitful figure in assignments to gather targeted information. This is not to say that you cannot or should not morally strict toward your children. The point is that you cannot be morally strict toward your job as a spy. The fact is: If you hate to lie, you cannot be a good spy.

6. **Live a low profile life.** If you want to be a full time secret agent, then your personal life should be low profile. The less known you are, the more effective you can be as a spy. The truth is, it is very hard or risky to keep a popular person working secretly (undercover). Governments and organizations in the past have used popular figures (dancers, actors, models, etc.) as spies-- but not full time.
(However, nowadays popular figures can work as full time spies via computer technology from safe places-- such as the operating of US drones or reading of people's emails).

7. **Master the art of fitting in.** The ability to fit in is one of the important three elements of your job as a spy. Your ability to fit in or blend in must be mastered. How? Practice on the different behaviours that go with different situations. How should you behave and look if you want to pretend as a religious man, business man (this will depend on the kind of business), a libertine, a drug dealer (this will depend of the kind of drug dealer you are pretending to be--a small dealer on the corner or a big wig?), a poor person, or a gay? Remember, you cannot use 'your' personality with your characters. Every assignment will require certain behaviour in order to fit in or blend in.

    There is difference between 'fit in' and 'blend in'. To fit in means to put on a behaviour and appearance well suited to the place and people you are carrying out an assignment amongst. To 'blend in' means to become unnoticeable. See the two examples below:

Example One (blend in): A husband suspects his wife is cheating and hires you to find out where she goes after work and who she meets. In this assignment you blend in (become unnoticeable) as you spy on her. To remain unnoticed, you will have to change your method (where you stand, when you drive, walk, ride) and also change your appearance (the clothes, hat, etc. you wear) each day you follow her.

The 'blend in' technique normally applies when you are following someone. You blend into the people around.

Example Two (fit in): The owner of a bar and restaurant is suspected of operating an illegal prostitution ring. Your assignment is to find out when these activities take place, who the women are, and the customers. In this assignment, you will have to fit in (put on a behaviour and appearance well suited to the bar & club) in order to do your job. You may have to pretend that you are--for example-- a guy named Mark Stewart when you get a job at the club. Or just Mark, if you will approach the club as a patron.

The 'fit in' technique applies to every assignment.

   8. **Your appearance must be changeable**. If you are a spy who goes on different assignments and have to use different fake identities, you should not have anything about your appearance that hinders you from making yourself look different. So avoid growing locks or beards that you are not willing to cut.

Assignments

As a spy, an assignment is any work you are hired to do. No matter for who, where, or how the assignment will be carried out, your main task is to gather information for whoever hires you. Here are some principles of assignments:

 Don't take any job.

 A spy that takes any job is not a cautious spy. You must have limitations in order to remain safe, wise, and only a spy. Assess every proposed job on the following criteria to decide whether or not you should take it on as an assignment:

 (a) <u>Risks.</u> What are the foreseen risks? Are you able to handle the risks? Do your research, give the proposed job some serious thought, and measure the risks against your capabilities to make a judicious decision on whether to take or refuse the job.

 (b) <u>Money.</u> How much the client can or is willing to pay? Are you comfortable with the payment? If you are self-employed, the amount of money you agree to take to do an assignment should be enough to cover the expected expenses you will incur carrying out the job, as well as enough for your bank account.

(c) <u>Tasks.</u> What exactly are you been asked to do? Your job as a spy is to gather information secretly. If you are asked to do something different, or additional, it may differ from the kind of spy that you are. You are still only a spy if an assignment involves a fourth element that requires you to purloin or destroy something. But if you take an assignment in which you are required to kill someone, then you are--in that particular assignment--an assassin. You are a spy, not a hired killer, and so you may want to refuse any job to kidnap or kill.

Clearly understand each assignment.

You must have a clear understanding of the nature of an assignment before you begin. If you work for a government or organization, it must explain clearly to you what you are required to do, the foreseen risks, how it will provide support to you on the assignment, the where and how, plus give you support in equipment and even other persons.

If you are self-employed, you should have discussion with your client to get all information necessary to facilitate your work. For example: If the owner of a large firm wants you to dig up information on the personal life of an employee, you will need to first get all the information the owner already has on that particular employee--such as name, date of birth, residential address, etc. You must also know exactly what the owner of the firm wants you to find in order to shape your work.

Be patient in an assignment.

Applying patience in every assignment makes you wise, work your way around dangers, and avoid failing an assignment. If a person or entity gives you an expected period to complete the job, this does not mean you should put aside patience. Using patience and diligence--not haste--is a part of a spy's discipline. Here is an example:

Example: Your assignment is to gather information on a particular lawyer's activities with a certain criminal. As part of the ways to do this, you decide to bug the lawyer's office. If you are impatient, you will think of 'breaking in'. If you are patient, you will think of 'getting in'. To get in, you may have to get a job at the office as a janitor or pose as a wealthy person seeking the service of the lawyer. Your research must be done to know the exact services provided by the lawyer.

How you will plant the bugging device depends a lot on the kind of device you are using. It is easier to bug a place with a listening device than with an audiovisual device. This is because audiovisual devices require proper positioning to properly capture the required images. With a small listening device on the other hand, you can simply bug the office desk while sitting there in front the lawyer and then find an excuse to leave.

Patience is the key. However, when time is against you, the option of breaking in, knocking someone out, creating distraction, etc., should be on the table.

Equipment and Weapons

To carry out an assignment, you need equipment or weapon. Some assignments require both. All secret agents need equipment and weapons. These are necessarily a part of the job. The choice of equipment and weapons to be used depends on the nature of an assignment.

Weapons.

Though you are only a spy--not an assassin, body guard or hit man-- your job still requires weapons. Your weapons do not have to be lethal (such as guns, knives, etc.) though they are very useful. Instead, the following weapons are highly effective:

Your mind. Your greatest weapon as a spy is your mind. No matter how physically fit you are, no matter the type of weapons you carry, if you are not quick to think yourself out of a perilous situation, you are too likely to fail. Always use your mind (craftiness) to get out of an uncomfortable or dangerous situation before trying anything else.

Your body. As a spy, you should train your body as a weapon. Learning techniques in self defence and attacks is vital.

Money and sex. Money and sex motivates individuals to act, at times foolishly. So you can use the power of money and sex to gain success in different assignments.

In terms of sex, you may have to--like James Bond--have sex with a particular individual as a way to accomplish your assignment. For example: Let's say your assignment is to gather information on behind the scene activities of a trading firm. So you get a job at the firm as a guy named Zack Weinberg. While working at the firm, the daughter of the CEO loves you (Zack) and wants a sexual affair. If you figure that getting close to her will get you close to the firm's records, to the owner of the firm, and even into the home and business conversations of the owner (CEO)--then go for it!

In terms of money, pretending as a wealthy figure, pretending as a person with the lack of money, or pretending as a person wanting to offer a lot of money for a particular illegal service, are just some ways you can use the power of money as a weapon to gain an advantage.

Laxative. This is an important weapon to use if you want to get a particular individual away in the bathroom long enough for you to steal something, break in, bug a place or do something else.

Sleeping pills. An important weapon to use in order to get someone unconscious long enough in order to carry out a search, remove something, etc.

<u>Nitrogen gas.</u> A quick weapon to get everyone in a room unconscious (or worse) in order to remove something---money, jewelry, etc.--from the room.

Equipments

The equipment you can use in your job as a spy are many. What you should use depend on an assignment.

Sun glasses.

The use of sun glasses is necessary when you are following someone or looking out for anything suspicious. But there are two significant rules that you must apply to the use of this equipment.

(a) **Avoid wearing sunglasses when there is no sun**. The use of sun glasses is common amongst spies and criminals. You would not 'fit in' if you are the guy in sun glasses in a restaurant across from the person you are spying on.

If you are following someone for a long time (more than one day, for example), you should not wear sun glasses all the time. You would not want to get noticed as the guy who is coming around in sun glasses. Don't draw suspicion on yourself.

(Sun glasses can do more than just hide your eyes. Sun glasses that voice record, video tape, or have X ray vision are ideal in some assignments).

<u>All communication equipment</u>

Communication is vital in your job. On or off an assignment, you must have a communication tool with you to contact a colleague, your client, and for others to reach you. Important communication equipment are:

(a) **Cell phones:** Not just any cell phone. You need a cell phone (smart phone) that can take pictures, video record, log you on to the internet, and read your geographical location. On some assignments, a regular-looking cell phone is not ideal. You will not be able to discreetly make a call or send a photo/text message in certain dangerous situations. This means that you will have to carry something that is a cell phone but doesn't look like a cell phone.

This is a watch that is also a cell phone with function of camera, image, video recorder, audio player, video clips, radio, recordings, equalizer and so on, very useful on dangerous assignments.

(b) Computer technology.

The use of computer technology to spy is wide in politics, business and private lives — such as the internet. Many persons nowadays use the internet to buy, sell and also send and store valuable information. Knowledge you have in the use of the internet can help you gather sensitive information in an assignment. It is also useful if you know someone, or few individuals, with knowledge in computer programming, software, encrypting, etc.

What to do if you are being followed by a car.

Let's say you are driving along and notice a black SUV shadowing you. We all know that general advice by cops--drive around, go to the nearest police station, etc. Well, that advice is not normally for a spy. The first thing you don't want to do is let the person following you knows that you know he is following you. So continue as normal. If the black SUV doesn't speed, you don't speed. If it doesn't come beside you, do not make any visible reaction. The first thing you should be using at this time is your mind--your greatest weapon. Gather enough information about the vehicle--licence plate, condition of the vehicle, face of the driver. Apart from losing the vehicle following you, you can call the police. Tell them that the black SUV is transporting illegal firearms. It is likely that the police will intercept them and get them of your trail. It doesn't matter that you have lied. Lying is a big part of your job. The important thing is that you have got rid of the follower.

Code Language

The use of codes in your job as a spy is a must. Passing on information in a code protects the information. Use code language in any form of communication--text, voice mail, phone calls, emails, letters, body language, etc.

It is wise that you create your own codes. Do not use codes that are already known, such as the following:

1. **Numbers to represent words**. This is a too common method of coding messages. The use of numbers to represent words (or vice versa) is too common nowadays. This form of coding is redundant in the job of a spy.

2. **Roman numbers to represent your own.** This also a too common form of coding. The use of Roman numbers to represent your own numbers or words is too weak for the job of serious espionage. While you could successfully code and send a piece of information using Roman numbers, the big question is: How are you going to avoid giving off the sign that you are using codes? Anyone who sees a writing of Roman numbers on a wall, on the ground, on a piece of paper, in a text message, email, etc. will most likely figure that it is a coded message.

3. **Foreign language.** Using a foreign language to code a communication is only sensible for some verbal communication. If you use it in writing, anyone can simply find an interpreter--or go to Google Translate--to decode the message. Imagine writing 'the Iranians will activate the bomb on December 31' in French. Too risky! Too foolish! While the Iranians may not understand French, it is easy for them to decode (translate) the message into their own language. Using a foreign language to code a piece of information in the world of espionage is also redundant.

4. **Sign language.** Using an established form of sign language to pass on information, to communicate, or to give an instruction, is not a wise thing in any situation. Coding with sign language works. But you will have to create your own form of sign language. For example: Your colleague knows that when you scratch your chin, you are sending the message that it is safe to make a particular move.

The most important coding rule:

When you code a piece of information, what you do is make the information secret, readable only by who understands the code. There is a most important rule about the use of codes:

Never let a code sound or look like a code. If a code language bears the sign of being a code, it will invoke the suspicion of others. This can be dangerous, especially in political espionage. Don't underestimate the intelligence of anyone. If you have sent, or were trying to send, a piece of information that does not make sense to the persons around you--they will figure that you are using codes.

So to prevent a code from bearing the sign of being a code, it must make sense. The information you are conveying must make a sense while carrying the secret message.

The following are two effective ways of sending information secretly:

Metaphors and hints. Sending information through metaphors and hints are very effective. For example, a spy is in the presence of some dangerous drug dealers in an assignment and he wants to tell his colleagues where he is over the phone. He decides to say the following:

"It is a windy day, baby.
 I now see no mud where I stand with you, only a large body of liquid and waiting boats to ride us on.
Girl, I love you."

The above coded information of the spy does two things: (a) It makes sense--the drug dealers standing by think he is talking with a girlfriend, (b) He uses metaphors to hint his location. His colleagues are also spies. So they know he is sending them information secretly. When they hear 'a windy day,' 'I now see no mud where I stand,' "a large liquid," and, "waiting boats," they will figure out that the spy is saying that he is by the sea. The fact that he says "waiting boats," means that he is standing by the sea where there are boats moored on shore.

Change the definition of words. This is another effective method of coding. By replacing the meaning of a word with another, you can easily send information secretly. For example: If you replace 'the President' with the term 'the garden' you make it easy to convey information about the President without arousing suspicion.

Things you should never do:

Never become a double agent.

This is a highly life-threatening thing to do. Germany, Russia, France, and the United States have--through history-- eliminated double agents. The only sensible personal motivation for becoming a double agent is greed.

Never use your real identity in all assignments.

This is because some dangerous assignments will require a fake identity in order to fit in or blend in and also protect you. Using your real identity (real name, address, age, facial looks, etc.) puts your real life at risk.

Never carry your real identification when acting under a fake identity.

This means that not carrying your real passport, drivers licence, national ID or any form of document that identifies the real you. Don't think of hiding your real drivers licence under the car seat. If someone decides to check you out, they may look there in their search.

Never let your fake identity looks too perfect.

When you create a fake identity for an assignment, the fake person you are portraying should not appear too perfect or faultless. For example: If you are pretending to be a guy named Joshua who has a moustache and walks with a limp, let Joshua have even one fault--such as fear of heights because he fell from a tree as a child. Persons are generally more connected to a humanly person. If Joshua appears too perfect, he will make others become curious and want to dig into his background.

Remember, one of the three elements of your job as a spy is to 'fit in,' so any fake identity you create must look somewhat normal within the surrounding that he operates. Even if a fake identity has to look very smart or very intelligent in order to fit in, he still should not appear too perfect.

Never leave your emotions open.

A spy must not be emotionally weak. Therefore, you must guard yourself against how you quickly respond to anything, any person or any situation that stimulates your emotion. This means that you should not be too quick to get sexually aroused by, say, a beautiful woman who approaches you: get distracted by, say, a commotion; get angry and say something you should not have said.

Things that you should do

Always have a backup plan.

You should never think that nothing can go wrong in your plan. Once you are taking a risk, the possibility that something may go wrong exist. Therefore you must always have a backup plan. A backup plan is a planned action you decide to take if the first fails.

In some situations, however, both the first plan and the backup plan may fail. In such an event, you must do what is must judicious--such as run, cause a distraction, knockout an individual, act unconscious, or hide.

Keep your job private.

You cannot tell your family, neighbours or best of friends that you are a spy. If you are self-employed, replace the word 'spy' and the word 'secret agent' with the term 'private investigator.' In this way you can simply say that you are a private investigator. But you should not go into the details of your job.

Live out of a bag on an assignment.

If you will do an assignment out of town, or out of your country, you should only bring the basic things. Do not carry lots of clothes and bags as if you are moving into a new home. If possible, carry no bags at all. If you work for a government or organization, it must handle the costs and arrangement of your clothes, travel, personal care items, and accommodation.

Always remain alert.

Keep your senses active at all times in any assignment. Something may go wrong at any time or something you need to see or hear may occur at any time. So remain alert at all times.

Use all your senses at all times.

Your job is to gather information. Therefore you should use all your senses to do this. You should gather information via hearing, seeing, smelling, tasting, and touching. But don't just wait with the hope that information you need will come to your senses. To gather information, you will have to--amongst other things--eardrop, shadow and peep.

Don't be quick to believe everything you hear.

A person or situation can be misleading. So do not be quick to believe. It is wise to treat every person and every situation with caution.

Always try to make evidence of information.

Just saying that you saw, you heard, are not always enough. Therefore it is wise--as much as possible-- to make evidence of information. This means you should make use of different evidence storing equipment--such as cameras, voice recorders, video recorders, thump drive, etc., as the assignment so requires.

Keep your lies simple.

In every assignment, you must keep your lies simple. What you don't want to do is tell so many lies that it becomes hard or impossible to keep track of them. If in an assignment you are pretending to be a guy named Jack, for example, only basic information about Jack you need others to know--name, where from, occupation, marital status, and also age. If someone needs to know more about Jack, Jack doesn't see the necessity for such discussion--unless that someone is essential in the assignment, such as being Jack's employer.

Always use disposable identities.

The fake identity that you use in an assignment must be successfully discarded after the assignment. For example: If you do an assignment pretending as a guy named Derrick Ford, Derrick Ford must not exists after the assignment ends.

This is why you should not use your real identity in many assignments, because you would not want to have a situation in which you have to live your life hiding your real identity-- because you have endangered it in an assignment.

The End